W9-AES-245

The
Yemassee
Lands

POEMS OF
BEATRICE RAVENEL

Beatrice Witte about 1890

Beatrice Witte Ravenel in the 1920's

The Yemassee Lands

POEMS OF

BEATRICE RAVENEL

🖋 🖋 🖋

Selected and Edited, with an Introduction by

LOUIS D. RUBIN, JR.

The University of North Carolina Press
Chapel Hill

CARL A. RUDISILL LIBRARY
LENOIR RHYNE COLLEGE

811.52
R 19 y
70702
July, 1970

Copyright © *1969 by*
The University of North Carolina Press
All rights reserved
Manufactured in the United States of America
Library of Congress Catalog Card Number 75-78862

Certain of the poems appearing in
this collection were originally
published in Poetry.

CONTENTS

The
Yemassee
Lands

POEMS OF
BEATRICE RAVENEL

INTRODUCTION

During the 1920's, as is well known, there was a literary Renascence in the Southern states of the American Union. For the first time in many decades, poetry and fiction written by Southern authors became of national and even international interest and importance. There were little poetry groups forming throughout the region, new literary magazines were founded here and there, and Southern writing graduated from the genteel idealism of local color into a medium whereby writers of intelligence and imagination wrote novels, stories, poems, and essays that readers of similar intelligence and imagination could take seriously.

In poetry, the chief centers seemed to be Nashville, Tennessee, and Charleston, South Carolina. In Nashville the young Fugitives—John Crowe Ransom, Allen Tate, Robert Penn Warren, Donald Davidson, Merrill Moore—were producing a magazine, *The Fugitive*, which soon won an international reputation. In Charleston, DuBose Heyward, Hervey Allen, and John

Bennett organized the Poetry Society of South Carolina, whose annual prize contests and lecture programs became widely known.

Among the Charleston poets was a lady in her fifties, Beatrice Ravenel. Though not closely identified with the Poetry Society, she served as an officer at first, attended its meetings and reading programs, and won several of its annual prizes. She published some of her poems in national magazines, and won a certain amount of renown, but when the Poetry Society entered into a decline in the late 1920's as Heyward began concentrating on fiction and playwriting and Allen left Charleston to write novels, Beatrice Ravenel's work dropped into obscurity.

The poetry of the leading Charleston poets—Heyward, Allen, Josephine Pinckney—has long been out of print, and is for the most part forgotten. The group did not have the staying power of the Nashville poets, several of whom went on to become and remain among the leading literary figures of the twentieth century. There were numerous reasons for the failure of the Charleston poetry to survive its time, the chief one being that at its best the Charleston poetry was noteworthy primarily for its novel use of the picturesque Carolina Low-Country locale, and attracted attention mostly because of that. Unlike Ransom, Tate, and Warren of Nashville, the Charleston poets were not vitally interested in language; their work exhibited little originality of diction or imagery. Since it is through its use of language that poetry survives its immediate occasion, the Charleston poetry was soon forgotten. Heyward today is remembered for writing the libretto of the folk-opera *Porgy*, and Allen for *Anthony Adverse*. John Bennett's early children's story, *Master Skylark*, still has some vogue. Otherwise the group is forgotten. The Poetry Society still exists, but its importance is now only local. As for Beatrice Ravenel, nothing of hers is still read today.

In 1928 the late Addison Hibbard published an anthology designed to show off the work of the best Southern poets. It was entitled *The Lyric South*, and contained poems by dozens of writers. Most of the poets and their poems have long since been forgotten, and for good reason. The greater part of the poetry in Hibbard's anthology is shallow, mannered, sentimental. Reading through the collection today, one finds very few memorable poems, or even lines: the verse of Ransom and Davidson stands out sharply (Tate and Warren did not have poems included.) The work of the other poets represented is sentimental, verbally uninteresting, very much dated forty years later—with one exception. There are five poems included by Beatrice Ravenel, and several of these alone show, of all the work by poets other than Ransom and Davidson, a lively imagination at work in the medium of language. In the poetry of Beatrice Ravenel, there is life in language, so that they read as well today as when *The Lyric South* was first published.

If one becomes interested in these poems, and secures a copy of her single book, *The Arrow of Lightning*, published in 1925, he will discover that her best work, however little noticed during the 1920's and thereafter, possesses a sturdiness, a quality of imagination, an excitement of imagery and diction, that are far superior to the work of any of the other Charleston poets. Her best poems are not only more interesting than those of DuBose Heyward, Hervey Allen, and Josephine Pinckney, they are better than any other poetry being written in the South during the 1920's outside of Nashville. They are, I think, worthy of lasting attention. They deserve to be anthologized, read, and remembered; they do not merit the oblivion that has been their fate. It is in the hope of stimulating renewed interest in the best work of a little-known but genuinely talented Southern poet that this volume is being published.

Because Beatrice Witte Ravenel is forgotten, except among those residents of Charleston who knew and remember her as a person, a biographical sketch is in order. She was born at 321 East Bay Street in Charleston, South Carolina, on August 24, 1870, the third of six daughters of Charles Otto and Charlotte Sophia Reeves Witte. A German, Witte came to America as a young man, setting up in New York in the importing business. In the 1840's he was sent down the Atlantic Coast to Charleston. He liked the city, settled there, married, went back to Germany immediately following the Civil War but returned afterward, and became an extremely successful banker. Witte possessed impressive wealth at a time when there was very little wealth in war-devastated Charleston. In 1879 he bought a large home at 112 Rutledge Avenue (now the Ashley Hall School for Girls), entertained widely, played an active role in community affairs, served as German and Scandinavian consul, and until his death in 1908 was among the most respected citizens of the city. His wife was from an old Charleston family of Huguenot ancestry, and the Wittes were a part of the city's social life—though Witte himself did not belong to the exclusive St. Cecilia Society, and his daughters were ineligible to attend the famous balls.

The Witte children were educated privately and at Miss Kelly's Female Seminary in Charleston, and as they grew into young womanhood, they became very much the center of admiration of the local society; there are still elderly residents of Charleston who remember the aura of the "Witte girls," all of them, in memory at least, brilliant and beautiful. Eventually all married well; Alice became the wife of Earle Sloan, a geologist; Fay married the journalist William Watts Ball, for many years editor of *The News and Courier* and author of *The State That Forgot,* a memoir of post-Reconstruction up-country South Carolina that is still widely cited by historians; Carlotta married Francis S. Van Boskerck, an officer in the U.S. Coast Guard; Belle married the prominent lawyer and banker Julian Mitchell; and Laura, the youngest, became the wife of Thomas R. Waring, editor of the *Charleston Evening Post.* At this writing Mrs. Ball is still alive, at the age of one hundred, Mrs. Van Boskerck, at ninety-six, and Mrs. Waring, at ninety-one.

Of the six Witte girls, it was Beatrice who was the intellectual. Her sister Laura wrote many years later, in memoir, that "Beatrice, dubbed the 'book worrum,' was giften with the brains of the family. Her father said her memory was colossal. She inherited that from him. She cared more for books and for reading than for other things, but she had a tremendous range of other interests, drawing and painting, writing plays and going with her friends. She could tell wonderful stories to the spellbound children. She had beautiful thick curly dark hair and blue eyes, and was always most vital and interesting." She began writing poetry quite early; her daughter has in her possession a small pamphlet, bound in ribbon, entitled "Christmas Poem, by Miss Beatrice B. Witte," with the further title of "Christmas Eve, Read before the Pupils of the Charleston Female Seminary, December 23rd, 1885."

Having completed the curriculum of the Female Seminary, Beatrice Witte might have been expected to enroll in one of the fashionable "finishing schools" which young Southern ladies of her day customarily attended. Instead, however, she applied for admission and was accepted at the Society for the Collegiate Instruction of Women of Cambridge, Massachusetts, known after 1893 as Radcliffe College, the women's division of Harvard University. She was a student there for three years, 1889-92, and in 1895 returned for two more years of work. She did not study for a degree, but took special courses, mostly in English, French, and German literature and philosophy.

Apparently she was as exciting a personality on the Harvard scene as in Charleston. She wrote for the *Harvard Monthly,* was one of its editors, published poems in the *Advocate,* and was one of a brilliant group of young men and women, including the Hapgood brothers, Norman and Hutchins, and the poets William Vaughn Moody and Trumbull Stickney, who cut a considerable figure in Cambridge intellectual circles. Norman Hapgood, soon to be famous as the editor of *Collier's* during its "muckraking" period, was very fond of her, as was his brother Hutchins, who later produced important studies of slum life in New York City. In his autobiography, *The Changing Years* (1930), Norman Hapgood wrote of her at the time:

At the [Harvard] Annex my friendships were highly intellectual. Always I have felt a need for the thought of women, alongside the thought of men. For a time the Harvard Monthly had an associate board of girls, to keep track of what was written in the Annex, and it included Beatrice Witte, now Beatrice Ravenal [sic], whose 'Poe's Mother' shows her quality in verse, as in prose she has shown it both in short stories and in editorials. Her fitness for editorials was indicated by the daily themes that were an outstanding element of our English work, and of one of her most-talked-of themes I was the butt. It was a picture of me as she saw me one day walking down Brattle Street, with a visiting young woman whom Beatrice described as a 'wily society girl,' who was going through the motions of intense interest in the soulful opinions I was pouring out, and the theme bore the ironical title of 'Sancta Simplicitas.'

Another engaging anecdote of Beatrice Witte at Harvard is furnished in Hutchins Hapgood's autobiography, *A Victorian in the Modern World* (1939). He describes the salon of a well-known Cambridge matron:

The house of Mrs. C. H. Toy stands out prominently in my remembered experience. Her husband was Professor of Semitic Languages in the university, and he was one of those scholarly, wise, sweet-tempered old men who always have had so much attraction for me. He had a spark of fire in his dark eyes: he was a Southerner and, on the surrender of Lee, was one of those who wished to retreat to the mountains and keep up guerilla warfare. His wife was very much younger, and I think it fair to say that she was the social leader of that part of the community. She loved to have the lions with her, and there the lions were either brilliant teachers or promising young students. She gave many successful dinners, where could be found William James, George R. Carpenter, George Santayana, to mention some of the well-known names; and dazzling young students like William Vaughn Moody, who at that time also showed his talent for poetry, and my brother Norman, much admired in the university; and Beatrice Witte, the most brilliant student at the Harvard Annex (afterward Radcliffe College).

Miss Witte was the only girl I remember in college who was noticeably gifted as a writer. She wrote for the *Harvard Monthly* and the *Advocate,* and was adored by young intellectuals like Norman, William Vaughn Moody, and Robert Lovett, whose enthusiasm for the forms of the mind enabled them to be attracted by superior girls. But Miss Witte was not only gifted mentally; she had an attractive and baffling personality, and was apparently lacking in the soft sentimentality which the superior young Harvard man disliked. One little incident illustrates the popularity which she justly held. William Vaughn Moody one evening took her out somewhere, probably to a concert, and they had a long walk home from Boston, but without exchanging a word. That was a sign of great superiority. But when they arrived at her house, Moody weakened sufficiently to say a bitter good night. "If you hadn't said that," remarked Miss Witte, "I would have had some respect for you."

Throughout this period she did much writing. Not only did she publish in the *Monthly* and the *Advocate,* but a short story, "A Case of Conscience," was accepted and published in *Scribner's Magazine,* and another, "A Little Boy of Dreams," appeared in the *Chap-book Magazine* and was reprinted in the second number of *Chap-book Stories,* an annual. Several poems appeared in a short-lived little magazine, *Knight Errant,* and an article in the *Harvard Monthly,* "The Coming Man in Fiction," was reprinted in part in *The Literary Digest.* Meanwhile she earned high grades from such scholars as William James, Barrett Wendell, George Lyman Kittredge, George Santayana, and George Pierce Baker, studying Elizabethan and nineteenth-century drama with Baker in the years just before he set up his famous '47 Workshop.

During these years she wrote the typical idealistic verse of the period; it was filled with poetic language, usually rhymed, and devoted almost exclusively to the subject of Love. To the selection of her poetry that follows I have added several of the best early lyrics, mainly to show the kind of verse she was then writing. Most of the early work was no worse and no better than most magazine verse of the 1890's, though occasionally it shows signs, despite its highly mannered diction, of an originality of language that in part redeems it from sentimentality. But if Beatrice Witte appeared notably free of soft sentimentality to the young Harvard intellectuals of the period, the poetry she was writing then is nevertheless mainly composed of just such sentiment.

What manner of poet Beatrice Witte might ultimately have become if, instead of returning home to Charleston, she had decided to remain in the Northeast, or perhaps go to England or the Continent for further study, it is impossible to say. She had talent, imagination, intelligence; among friends, some of whom later became important literary figures, she was highly respected. But few young women of good family did such things in the 1890's, especially if they were from an old Southern city such as Charleston. Whether she ever considered remaining in the North and pursuing a literary or academic career, there is no evidence one way or the other; very probably her family would have opposed it if she had proposed doing so. (One suspects that Norman Hapgood would not have been uninterested in her staying in the North, to judge from several of his letters of some years later.) There is, however, no indication that she went back to Charleston reluctantly. For by that time she had met Frank Ravenel.

A year older than she, Francis Gualdo Ravenel (1869-1920) was a tall, good-looking young man, cultivated and witty, with what DuBose Heyward later described as a "peculiarly endearing charm of manner." His mother, Harriet Horry Ravenel, was a writer of some note, who was author of a biography of Eliza Lucas and a volume of social history, *Charleston, the Place and the People* (1906). Though of distinguished social position,

Frank Ravenel, like many another young Charlestonian, was very poor. They were married in 1900, and it was emphatically a love match; a little poem written in the early 1920's after Frank Ravenel died, entitled "Salvage" (p. 65), is evidence enough of that. Upon his death in 1908, C. O. Witte had left some $250,000 to his daughter, a highly respectable dowry indeed for Charleston at the time. Apparently Frank Ravenel invested most of it in real estate operations, all of which proved notably unsuccessful, for by the middle 1910's the Ravenels had very little money, and the income that Beatrice Ravenel began earning from the writing of magazine fiction was an important part of the family's budget. For some years the three Ravenels —a daughter, Beatrice St. Julien, was born in 1904—lived at Ocean Plantation, which despite its imposing name was a swampy farm in the low country south of Charleston. It is very probably the locale for one of Beatrice Ravenel's best poems, "The Alligator" (pp. 33-36).

During all this time, she wrote almost no poetry. From 1902 to 1917 her manuscript book shows only one lyric which she apparently considered significant enough to copy out. It was not until 1917 that she began writing verse again to any extent, seemingly moved to do so by the emotional impetus of the American entry into World War I. A friend showed some of her new poems to the editor of *The Atlantic Monthly*, who accepted several, whereupon she began once again writing poetry in earnest. It was at this time, too, that for financial reasons she began turning out popular magazine fiction. Most of it was published in *Ainslie's*, for which she continued to write up through 1925. Other stories appeared in *Harper's* and *The Saturday Evening Post*. One, "The High Cost of Conscience," was reprinted in the *O. Henry Memorial Prize Stories* for 1919.

In 1919, too, Mrs. Ravenel began writing editorials and other articles for the Columbia, S.C., *State,* of which her brother-in-law, William Watts Ball, was the editor. Her speciality was foreign affairs, and evidently she possessed a skill that ran above the usual standards of newspaper editorial writing, if we are to judge from something that Norman Hapgood wrote to her, and also mentioned in his autobiography. In 1922, he informed her in a letter, he was dining with the columnist "F.P.A.," Franklin P. Adams of the New York *World,* and the conversation turned to editorial writing. "I said there were only two—possibly four— good editorial writers in America," Hapgood wrote, "and I named them. He said, 'I have found another. I noticed certain editorials in the Columbia State and wrote to the editor about them. They were by a woman named Ravenel.' He pronounced it Rayvanel.

> " 'What is her first name?'
> " 'I don't know.'
> " 'Is it Beatrice?'
> " 'Yes. That is it.' "

The poetry that Beatrice Ravenel began writing again, though it was published in good magazines, represented little technical advance at first over what she had done back at Harvard in the 1890's; it was highly abstract and very sentimental. One poem, "Missing," first published in *The Atlantic,* was subsequently reprinted in several collections; a war poem, it is full of the patriotism of popular verse of the period, and its renown was no doubt due to its theme. I have not included it in this collection.

Apparently, however, in writing and publishing poetry again, Mrs. Ravenel also began paying serious attention to what was being written by good poets of her own time. She subscribed to *The Dial* during its most brilliant years, the early 1920's, which coincided with her own renewed development. The shock of her husband's death in 1920 also doubtless had its effect on her work. In any event, with her formidable intelligence and her feeling for language, she was not long in perceiving the defects of her verse. For in 1920 and 1921 there is an abrupt and startling change in her writing. It is as if she had come upon the poetry of Amy Lowell, the Imagists, and other moderns, and suddenly realized what it was possible to do with language in a poem, whereupon she began doing it. Almost overnight she put aside the sentimental ideality of the poetry of the waning genteel tradition, with its poetic abstractions, ornate and artificial literary language, and its strained diction, and began writing in free verse, with notable economy of diction, a sharp precision of language, and vivid, evocative imagery. In the poems that now followed, she began utilizing her intelligence to the fullest extent, producing verse that conceded nothing in richness of vocabulary and complexity of thought.

It is likely, as H. Morris Cox suggests in his doctoral dissertation on the Charleston poets, that the coming into being of the Poetry Society of South Carolina in 1920-21 also had much to do with this abrupt development in Mrs. Ravenel's poetry. She was not among its immediate founders, but was elected to its first executive committee, and was affected by the general interest in contemporary poetry that the formation of the Society helped to stimulate. One notes that during the first year of the Society's existence, among the poets brought to Charleston to give readings was Carl Sandburg, whose well-known use of vers libre must have interested Mrs. Ravenel. But there is little real affinity of attitude there; it seems more likely that Amy Lowell and the Imagists proved more useful to her. The main influence of the Poetry Society upon her work was probably that it set Charleston to talking about, reading, and writing poems.

In 1922, the second year of the Society's existence, Amy Lowell came to Charleston to read, and met Mrs. Ravenel. They spent some hours with each other, and a correspondence ensued which continued through the remainder of Miss Lowell's life. In the quite feminine, yet intense and intellectually bold personality of Amy Lowell, Beatrice Ravenel found someone who understood what she was doing, and apparently the same was true for Miss Lowell, who wrote often and referred once to "that odd something which makes one person sympathetic to another." The letters they wrote are lengthy, expressive, and affectionate.

Mrs. Ravenel evidently mentioned to Miss Lowell that she hoped to bring out a book of her verse, for Miss Lowell asked to examine the manuscript, went through seventy-one poems, and rated them from "excellent" to "poor." "Certainly you have a very rare and unusual talent," she wrote, "but it does not seem to me that you are quite critical enough of your own work yet." The manuscript included a number of the earlier poems as well as her most recent work in free verse, and Miss Lowell noted that the work seemed to break into two distinct halves. "Metre seems to put your whole mood backward into an earlier time," she wrote, "and the particular touch which you show in your later poems is not present in most of these poems which are written in metre. . . . One of the objections to the metrical poems is your tendency to lapse into the old, discarded poetical jargon with 'these' and 'thous' and 'haths' and 'arts.' There is a leaning toward the merely pretty and sentimental in these metrical poems which lies in wait for you when you write metre, and which is entirely absent in your cadenced verse." The poems that Amy Lowell liked and thought worth publishing were numerous; she singled out for special praise "The Yemassee Lands," which she said was superb, and offered to recommend a manuscript of the best poems to the Houghton Mifflin Company.

Meanwhile "The Yemassee Lands" had won the Poetry Society Prize of the Poetry Society of South Carolina for 1922, and was published in the *Year-book*. Mrs. Ravenel now proceeded to produce a number of her best poems, which were published in various magazines. Her book manuscript, which she entitled *The Arrow of Lightning,* was offered to several commercial publishers, but was turned down, and eventually it was brought out by the young publisher Harold Vinal in 1925, with Mrs. Ravenel bearing part of the expense. For the sake of Beatrice Ravenel's contemporary reputation it was doubtless unfortunate that Amy Lowell died before the book was published; certainly she would have seen to it that *The Arrow of Lightning* received attention from critics and reviewers. As it was, the volume earned almost no national notice.

Though Beatrice Ravenel continued to write poetry for several decades, she published little of it, never brought out another book collection, and except for occasional republication of poems in a few anthologies and textbooks, dropped out of public notice as a poet. In 1926 she was married again, and to another Ravenel. Her second husband, Samuel Prioleau Ravenel, was only distantly related to her first husband; his family was originally Charlestonian, but he was born in Paris, where his family had removed following the Civil War. A lawyer, he had lived for a number of years in Asheville, North Carolina. With her second marriage, Beatrice Ravenel's need to support herself and her daughter through journalism and fiction writing ended. During the late 1920's and the 1930's the Ravenels traveled extensively. Mrs. Ravenel now produced little poetry, though she wrote one group of poems, based on the West Indies, unpublished during her lifetime, which are among her best work. Samuel Prioleau Ravenel died in Charleston in 1940. Beatrice Ravenel resided there, in the house at 126 Tradd Street where her daughter still lives, for the rest of her life. She continued to read extensively. One of her favorite authors was William Faulkner, whose work she admired from the first, even when he was considered a scandalously sensational author. Her daughter recalls that the Charleston Free Library, after complaints from members, refused to add additional Faulkner novels to its collection, and when Mrs. Ravenel sent her daughter to find a new Faulkner work, the librarian at the desk "slammed me down."

In 1956, at the age of eighty-five, Mrs. Ravenel died.

Of the poems that Beatrice Ravenel wrote during the 1920's, among the best, I believe, are those that make up a three-part work having to do with the Indian past of the Carolina Lowcountry. Though Beatrice Ravenel did not draw on locale for its immediate exotic and picturesque uses, as her Charleston contemporaries were accustomed to doing, most of her best work arises out of her strong sense of place and of history. She was, in the best sense of the word, a provincial poet. She possessed, as Morris Cox has noted, a kind of historical sensibility that went beyond the mere recital of incidents and events from the past. "The Yemassee Lands" and its two companion poems "The Alligator" and "The Arrow of Lightning" take for their basic theme the presence, in the Carolina Low-Country of two hundred years previous, of the Yemassee Indians, and of their subsequent dispersal and extinction. William Gilmore Simms had used the same subject for one of his best novels, *The Yemassee* (1835); Mrs. Ravenel was clearly familiar with it—most of the Indian lore in her poems is drawn from that in *The Yemassee*, which Simms invented for the occasion—and also with some of the historical accounts of the Yemassees and their final raid on the English settlements near Charleston which resulted in their defeat and ultimate extinction. In the three poems she is concerned with the unchanging forests and swamps of the Low-country, and the contrast between human notions of time and that embodied in the natural world, as manifested in the complete disappearance of the Yemassees and the coming of the white man's civilization, while the locale remains intact. "The Arrow of Lightning" begins with the poet's being awakened at night by the song of a mockingbird:

> Out of the dark of the moon, a resistless fountain,
> Sweeter than water, sweeter than running water,
> The music drags me from sleep.

One detects, here as throughout the three-part Yemassee poems, a strong flavor of Walt Whitman; she uses the cadenced patterns, the lines of uneven length patterned by internal assonance and consonance, the repetition of key words and of units of rhythm within lines and stanzas, that are typical of Whitman. It was Whitman who, more than any other poet, seems to have spoken most strongly to Mrs. Ravenel's imagination.

The immediate reactions to the bird's song are thoughts of

conventional, literary emotion that are seemingly appropriate to the occasion: " 'My heart aches . . . embalmèd darkness' . . . / 'Listen, Eugenia . . . Eternal passion—eternal pain!' . . ." But, she muses, why should the song of the mockingbird be conceived of in such conventional terms, when the actual woods and swamps where the bird is singing contain memories of a history that is much more immediate and meaningful?

> Oh, what have you had to do
> With English wood-rides,
> Trees pampered like the horses in a stall?
> Why intellectualize your savagery
> With velvet turf that almost bears the arcs
> Of scarlet heels?
> You sing of a terrible land,
> A lapsing, sea-enthralled, sleep-walking land,
> For miles without a pebble or a rock— . . .

On its wings the mockingbird bears the "v" marking that was the Yemassee totem, the arrow of lightning, and the bird, known to the Indians as "trick-tongue," is as wild as the red men once were:

> Mocking-bird! Trick-tongue!
> Tuft of the arrow, the Arrow of Lightning, the keen
> And flashing totem of the Yemassee,
> Is struck on your wings!
> The flying point is vibrant in your voice.
> You are a warrior;
> Shrieking your scalp-song, you dart into the faces
> Of birds and monstrous cats,
> Giants that flatten haunches into the cowering grass,
> Cowards, whose whiskers tremble like the sentimental
>   blown antennae
> Of wild azaleas,
> Before your furious passion.

Though the Yemassees are long since gone, and "Torches are quenched / In the running of water," the bird sings on, of

a country
Where love is more savage, more unappeasable
Than storm from the wild Caribbean,
Gentler than petals of trembling mimosa,
And sings in the dark of the moon.

There must be language, she thinks, that can describe that time when the Indian tribes occupied the land, and how they left, and therefore of time, change, the ephemerality of men, and the passion of love. There must be words

To tell of the passing of nations,
Of the exquisite ruin of coasts, of the silvery change and
the flux of existence,
And of love that remakes us—

Trick-tongue!

Selecting words carefully, avoiding the easy abstractions of local color poetry, Mrs. Ravenel portrays, in the song of the mocking-bird, the Indian memories in the forest and the lush, verdant, savage natural beauty of the Low-country swamps. She does not commit the error of romanticizing the bird's song, by pretending that the mockingbird itself is saying these things: she makes it clear from the outset that these are her musings on what the bird's song means.

The second poem in the sequence, "The Alligator," which I think one of Mrs. Ravenel's very best poems, builds upon the same theme. She begins with the sound of an alligator in the thickets of the Low-country:

He roars in the swamp.
For two hundred years he has clamored in Spring;
He is fourteen feet long, and his track scars the earth in
the night-time,
His voice scars the air.

The raw bellow of the alligator is juxtaposed with the profusion of color and brightness of the Low-country in the springtime, in a fine stanza in which the scene is vividly recreated in language:

Oak-boughs have furred their forks, are in velvet;
Jessamine crackle their fire-new sparks;
The grass is full of a nameless wildness of color, of
flowers in solution.
The glass-blower birds twist their brittle imaginings
over the multiplied colors of water.

The intensity and prolixity of the imagery shows how vital and complex Mrs. Ravenel's language can be. Her imagery here is startling both in its richness and in its intellectuality: to liken the songs of birds in a swamp to the blowing of glass is something that would not have occurred to her fellow South Carolina poets, and is emblematic of the manner in which her best poetry rises, through its boldness of language and thought, above the conventional generalities of local color.

"But the counterpoint of the Spring," she continues, is the alligator's cry, "Exacerbate, resonant, / Raw like beginnings of worlds," which expresses a vitality that is animal, masculine, primitive:

A thing in itself,
Not only alive, but the very existence of death would be
news to it.
Will—
Will without inflexion,
Making us shudder, ashamed of our own triviality—
The bull alligator roars in the swamp.

Having depicted the alligator's cry in counterpoint to the luxurious growth and brightness of the swamp in springtime, she then changes the mood abruptly, to describe the way in which the swamp presents itself to humans who live at its edge:

This is queer country.
One does not walk nor climb for a view;
It comes right up to the porch, like a hound to be patted.
Under our hog-back

The swamp, inchoate creature, fumbles its passage, still
    nearer;
Puffing a vapor of flowers before it.

She notes the changing condition of the swamp from week to
week. One week, she says, the woods are full of ponds reflecting
the sky; the next week the ponds may evaporate, leaving foot-
paths of mud in which trapped fish may be "gasping, baffled in
in semi-solids." Then she returns to the sounds, which seem as
thick as the mud to the trapped fish, "Thick-blooded compulsive sound," which "Like scum in the branch, chokes, mantles
the morning." And this time she likens the cry of the bull alligator to what Simms had depicted as the ancient war-cry of the
Yemassee: "*Sangarrah! . . . Sangarrah! . . . Sangarrah! . . .*"

Two hundred years previously, she imagines, an Indian
medicine man sat holding a young alligator, reciting "the secret
name, the name of the Manneyto, / *Y-O-He,* / Never known by
the people." The medicine man pronounced the name of the
Indian God to the alligator, tracing on its serried back the shape
of a sharp-curved arrow, calling the alligator's name: " 'Nanneb-
Chunchaba, / Fish-like-a-Mountain, / Remember!' " The Yemassees, he says, are leaving the land, their hunting grounds fallen
to the white man: "In the hills of our dead, in the powdering
flesh that conceived us, / Shall the white man plant corn." The
very memory of the Yemassees will soon be erased from the
swamp. The medicine man himself will be buried here before
the Indians leave, and will be forgotten:

I shall hide from them all, as the war-chiefs
Cover their lives with the tree-tops,
Leaving them safe when they go on the war-path.
I shall sleep in this place.

In days to come, when the voice of the Indians will be gone,
"Speak for the Yemassee!", he instructs the small alligator:

Nanneb-Chunchaba, you, little Fish-like-a-Mountain,
Shout through the forest the terrible war-cry of
    Yemassee!

"Sangarrah! . . . Sangarrah-me! . . . Sangarrah-me!
Shout! I shall hear you!
Sangarrah! . . ."

Thus the command given by the Indian medicine man to the
alligator in the swamp, and which it now fulfills:

> For two hundred years—
> Will, without inflexion—
> The bull alligator
> Roars from the swamp
> In the Spring.

Closing with the same incident that began the poem, the cry of
the bull alligator itself, she uses it to symbolize the pure physi-
cality of spring in the swamp, and to evoke the memory of the
region's past, and to contrast the unthinking, savage, natural
vigor of the life of the swamp with the tenuous concerns that
motivate men.

In the final poem of the sequence, "The Yemassee Lands,"
the historical memory of the Indians, suggested in "The Arrow of
Lightning," imagined in "The Alligator," now comes back until
it is foremost in the mind of the observer, and the Indians are
all but actually present. Taking for her scene the bending course
of the Savannah River through the Low-country, she divides her
poem into nine numbered stanzas, each a different view of the
river's path through the lands once owned by the Yemassees.
In the opening stanzas, though the river winds through the
Yemassee country and one momentarily expects the Indians
themselves to appear, they do not show themselves:

> Always, just round the turning, the stealthy canoe
>   with its naked, upstanding warrior
> Comes . . . for the wild-fowl rise in a hurtling of
>   startled feathers;
> Never comes into sight.

But the ground at the edge of the swamp seems to reiterate
their presence, as "liquid gold" orchids "bend from cylindrical

sheaths / Under a phantom moccasined tread," and by the fourth stanza, the pine trees

> stand with scarlet and quivering outlines—
> Initiate boys whose whipped young blood leaps up
> Now, the first time, to the war-path.
> Shadows of red, shadows of bronze and of copper
> Disengage from the wood-growth;
> One after one, the long, lithe, menacing war-line
> Loops through the stems.
> Light cups the crouching knees,
> Splinters on polished shoulders,
> Ravels in towering head-plumes.

The Indians still survive in the spirit of the land, and now have come back "When with blowing of wood-smoke and throbbing of hidden drums / Indian Summer fashions its spell, / Trembling falls on the air." The forest seems, in its very silence, to be filled with the imagined presence of the Yemassees, so that "Something follows and waits . . . / And will not be appeased." In autumn the storm winds bend and twist the trees until they are like horses "Tossing their frantic forelocks," which "Flee from the rush / Of invisible hunters." At night the "Stars in the coppery after glow of the sundown / Hang like strings of teeth on the savage breast of a warrior," the water-willows along the river trail in the current, "Draggle like scalps from the war-belt," while "the night-wind sings overhead / Like arrows on deadly sendings. . . ." The land is vibrant with the presence of the Indians, its earth troubled from the "thud of the young men's dances"; the thickets appear thick with hands that reach out for the scalp, and a pine tree struck by lightning and set afire "blazes with hideous cracklings, / Remembering the long black tresses of captive squaws / Tied to the death-pyre."

So that finally, to the modern observer who contemplates the forest and its imagined consciousness, the Yemassee Indians have returned to their lands, and remain there. They have become as one with the weather, and through the procession of the seasons they bespeak their impact:

> After two hundred years
> Has the forest forgotten?
> Always the trees are aware
> (Significant, perilous, shaken with whispers of dread
>   and of welcome)
> Of the passage of urgent feet.
> Violent shoots strain up to the air and the sunshine
> Of cut-over land;
> Leaves crowd over the barrows of last year's skeleton
>   leaves.
> Ever and ever again
> The Red Man comes back to his own
> In the Yemassee Lands.

The three Yemassee poems, it seems to me, are as effective a use of locale and of history as exists in Southern poetry. They demonstrate the quality of Beatrice Ravenel's art at its best. A subject that might have been so easily sentimentalized, and presented as merely picturesque and quaint, has been set forth concretely and vividly, in its own right, with the images and metaphors containing, and not merely alluding to, the meaning. What is most striking is the choice and use of words, the sensuous, evocative recreation of mood in language. The imagery is alive and functional, not sterile and merely ornamental. Few Southern poets, for example, could, in seeking to show the presence of the Yemassees in the thickets of Indian Summer, come up with the verb that Mrs. Ravenel chose for this image: "Out of the snarling keen-toothed vines / Berries wink with the cunning obsidian gleam / Of the arrow-head . . ." Such use of animate words to convey the inanimate movement of light on the vines, so as to suggest the imagined Indians, is quite beyond what her Charleston colleagues were capable of. The entire sequence shows not only a remarkable eye for descriptive imagery and a grasp of the sensuous properties of words, but a restraint of diction, a freedom from clichés and from empty, emotive abstractions that permit the poems to speak for themselves, and to depend for their success not upon the preconceived attitude of the reader to the theme, but upon the creativeness inherent in the language and imagery. A poem in other words, does not stand for a Poetic Idea; it *is* a poem. It is precisely this quality, I believe, that typifies the best work of Beatrice Ravenel. A craftsman with words, she wrote, in her best poems, lines and stanzas that avoid almost entirely the sentimental abstraction that is the bane of so much second-rate poetry during the dwindling but—in the 1920's and 1930's —still formidable tradition of genteel idealism in Southern poetry.

It is not without relevance, I think, that Beatrice Ravenel was university trained. Her work displays an unabashed use of the intellect, and is not content with the easy poetic phrases and undemanding language of so much Southern verse. Her poems are not over-simplifications of their subjects; they are not "written down." Consider, for example, her description, in a poem entitled "The Humming-Bird," of a summer garden after the rain:

> Clear, precise as an Audubon print,
>> The air is of melted glass,
>> Solid, filling interstices
> Of leaves that are spaced on the spines
>> Like a pattern ground into glass . . .

Then she describes the hummingbird

> Splitting the air, keen as a spurt of fire shot from the
>> blowpipe,
> Cracking a star of rays; dives like a flash of fire,
> Forked tail lancing the air, into the immobile trumpet;
> Stands on the air, wings like a triple shadow
> Whizzing around him.

There is a precision, a concrete specificity of language and imagery, here that are possible only because the poet knew that the connotative properties of words, and not Poetic Ideas, are what make a poem stay alive.

In some of Mrs. Ravenel's later poetry there is a directness and even a sensuality that is startling to come upon in the verse of a middle-aged Charleston lady. This is especially evident in a group of poems having to do with the West Indies, written apparently during the 1940's and not published during her lifetime. "At the Sacré Coeur in Paris / They took me for white," begins one lyric entitled "Jeune Fille Octoroon." It is about a half-breed girl educated in convent schools in Paris where in an art class the students were made to "swear in the chapel / Never to work in a life class / Where the models went without robes." But now comes temptation: ". . . the air of tonight / Is pressing against my body, / Insistent, harsh as a thorn-bush, / Saying, What can be this?" and the poem concludes with the native drums thumping, "abroad in this air, / Crying! Crying! Tearing the gauze of dusk / In the grove of the plunging shadows." In another such poem, "Love Song," a woman thinks that "My blood is caught in my veins as the fish is caught in the net. / The seine of my veins all over my body is full of the struggle, the gasp and the anguish. / Don't be afraid." The entire group of West Indian poems, which seem to have been the last that Mrs. Ravenel wrote, represent a sophistication of technique and language and a freshness of subject matter that are not only quite unlike anything else being written in Charleston at the time, but are among the more interesting work being done in American poetry of the period. Written as they were when the poet was in her sixties and even her seventies, they make one realize anew what kind of talent Mrs. Ravenel possessed, and what kind of work she might well have done under circumstances that could have kept her in contact with the more active and exciting currents of literary thought during the years when the lineaments of modern American poetry were coming into being.

The relevance of these poems, then, is twofold. First of all, they are eminently worth reading and preserving, I think, because of their solid achievement; they are among the most interesting work done by Southern poets during the 1920's and 1930's, and they constitute a small but significant addition to the body of distinguished poetry produced during the Southern Literary Renascence. The poems are sometimes sentimental; comparatively few poems are entirely free from that pervasive vice of most Southern verse. But I do think that her best poems are marked by an imaginative use of language and a boldness of metaphor and thought that set them apart from the mere local color pleasantries of most twentieth-century Southern poetry, and they do not therefore date but remain fresh and vital. The Yemassee poems, and some eight or ten of the others, constitute distinguished achievement in verse, and merit inclusion in any anthology of the best Southern poetry.

A second aspect of the interest inherent in Mrs. Ravenel's verse, it seems to me, lies both in what it is and is not. In its accomplishments and its unevenness, her poetry can be said to represent a fascinating "might-have-been," an example of what was possible and impossible to a genuine talent which, during the years that should have been the most creative of all, remained in comparative isolation from the mainstream of literary thought. This question presents itself: given Beatrice Witte Ravenel's talent, what kept her from developing into the poet she might have become? What was there about her circumstance —that of a young woman of good family growing up in an old, conservative Southern seaport community, and after a five-year stay at Harvard marrying and remaining very much a part of that society, so that throughout her twenties, thirties, and her forties she was isolated from almost all of the ideas, interests, and attainments of the most vital literature of her day—what was it that would not let her break loose, or even *want* to break loose?

It is an interesting problem in Southern cultural and social history, with implications for anyone who would seek to understand the region and its literature. No one would project so simple a causal explanation of what produces important writers as that of the mere environmental presence or absence of certain factors in the writer's immediate circumstance. Yet the social question does indeed arise, and students both of Southern literature and of the whole business of the causes, conditions, and psychology of literary creativity may find ground for speculation in Beatrice Ravenel's poetry.

What follows, then, is a selection of Mrs. Ravenel's verse. I have grouped it in four parts: poems published in *The Arrow of Lightning* and representing the bulk of her achievement during the 1920's, poems written subsequent to that book, the group of West Indian poems, and several early poems composed during or shortly after her years at Harvard. The choices throughout are my own; the volume is admittedly a selection. I have included one of the poems from *The Arrow of Lightning*, that entitled "Poe's Mother," because it was frequently reprinted in anthologies during the 1920's and was widely admired; I do not myself think it among her best work. Except for that, and for the several early poems, the selection that follows are those of Beatrice Ravenel's poems that I think are her best, and which stand up best several decades after their original composition. It is my hope that the appearance of these poems, long after most of them went and remained out of print, and at a time when there is deservedly so much interest in the literature written in the South during the twentieth century, may help to secure for them, and for their author, some of the notice and the respect that I think is so well merited.

In the preparation of this book I have had the considerable help of Beatrice Ravenel's daughter, Miss Beatrice St. Julien Ravenel, of Charleston, S.C., and an author in her own right. Not only did she transcribe all of her mother's unpublished work for me, but she furnished me with copies of the extensive correspondence from Amy Lowell and with much other material as well. I should like also to acknowledge the assistance of Mrs. Shannon Ravenel Purves, of the Houghton Mifflin Company, who on a visit to Charleston traced down a great deal of biographical information for me, and helped me with the preparation of my introduction. Professor Hennig Cohan of the University of Pennsylvania gave the manuscript a useful and sympathetic reading. Mr. Thomas R. Waring, Jr., editor of the Charleston *News and Courier,* provided me with much helpful information about his aunt, Mrs. Ravenel. My friend Caroline Triest, librarian of the High School of Charleston, assisted me, as she has often done before, in locating material. Professor H. Morris Cox, of Clemson University, made available to me his authoritative doctoral dissertation, "The Charleston Poetic Renascence, 1920-1930." Mrs. Eleanor Hewitt-Myring, daughter of the late W. W. Ball, kindly gave me permission to examine the Ball papers at the Duke University Library. Her sister, Mrs. Margaret Ball Hickey, also helped me in my search. Mrs. Woodrow M. Donovan, curator of manuscripts of the Radcliffe College Archives, furnished me with a complete account of Beatrice Witte's academic career.

In preparing the manuscript, I have silently emended occasional inconsistencies of spelling.

Louis D. Rubin, Jr.

University of North Carolina at Chapel Hill
July 15, 1968

PART ONE

From *The Arrow of Lightning*

THE ARROW OF LIGHTNING

Out of the dark of the moon, a resistless fountain,
Sweeter than water, sweeter than running water,
The music drags me from sleep.

Swimming through shallows of dreams
To a ready-made rapture . . .
"My heart aches . . . embalmèd darkness." . . .
"Listen, Eugenia . . .
Eternal passion—eternal pain!" . . .

Oh, what have you to do
With English wood-rides,
Trees pampered like the horses in a stall?
Why intellectualize your savagery
With velvet turf that almost bears the arcs
Of scarlet heels?
You sing of a terrible land,
A lapsing, sea-enthralled, sleep-walking land,
For miles without a pebble or a rock—
Only a silver shape—
To hold its loveliness against the sea.
A land that every Spring storms out in flowers,
Mad with forgetting, with the inundation of the moment
Saved from uncertainty.

You are no dryad,
No young squaw of trees;
You are a conjurer.
You sing the songs of all birds with a difference,
Bringing the drop of blood, the touch of dead man's fingers,
That makes the alchemy.

Mocking-bird! Trick-tongue!
Tuft of the arrow, the Arrow of Lightning, the keen
And flashing totem of the Yemassee,
Is struck upon your wings!

The flying point is vibrant in your voice.
You are a warrior;
Shrieking your scalp-song, you dart into the faces
Of birds and monstrous cats,
Giants that flatten haunches into the cowering grass,
Cowards, whose whiskers tremble like the sentimental
    blown antennae
Of wild azaleas,
Before your furious passion.

But this is the time of flowers.
The warrior slips through the trees on the trail of no lynx,
    of no panther, no ocelot.
The wand of the god Checkamoysee, the love-god,
    is broken,
Torches are quenched
In the running of water.
Sweeter than water, sweeter than running water,
You sing of a country
Where love is more savage, more unappeasable
Than storm from the wild Carribean,
Gentler than petals of trembling mimosa,
And sings in the dark of the moon.

There must be words of Catawba,
Barbed musical words of the Seminole,
Words of the wind
Weaving its Indian baskets of russet trash at the foot of
    the pine-tree,
To tell of the passing of nations,
Of the exquisite ruin of coasts, of the silvery change and
    the flux of existence,
And of love that remakes us—

Trick-tongue!

THE ALLIGATOR

He roars in the swamp.
For two hundred years he has clamored in Spring;
He is fourteen feet long, and his track scars the earth in the
  night-time,
His voice scars the air.

Oak-boughs have furred their forks, are in velvet;
Jessamine crackle their fire-new sparks;
The grass is full of a nameless wildness of color, of flowers
  in solution.
The glass-blower birds twist their brittle imaginings over
  the multiplied colors of water.

But the counterpoint of the Spring—
Exacerbate, resonant,
Raw like beginnings of worlds,
Cry of the mud made flesh, made particular, personal,
Midnight assailing the morning, myopic sound, blinded
  by sun,—
Roars from the swamp.
A thing in itself,
Not only alive, but the very existence of death would be
  news to it.
Will—
Will without inflexion,
Making us shudder, ashamed of our own triviality—
The bull alligator roars in the swamp.

This is queer country.
One does not walk nor climb for a view;
It comes right up to the porch, like a hound to be patted.
Under our hog-back
The swamp, inchoate creature, fumbles its passage, still
  nearer;
Puffing a vapor of flowers before it.

This week there are ponds in the wood, vertiginous skies
    underfoot,
Pondering heaven.
Next week, in the pashing mud of the footpath
Fish may be gasping, baffled in semi-solids.
The negroes will eat them.

This is queer country.
Thick-blooded compulsive sound,
Like scum in the branch, chokes, mantles the morning.

Sangarrah! . . . Sangarrah! . . . Sangarrah! . . .

Two hundred years back—
And the medicine-man of the Yemassee
Sat in the thick of the swamp, on the ridge where the
    cypresses flung
Their elfin stockade.
Wrinkled his chest as the cast-off skin of the blacksnake,
The hide of his cheeks hung square and ridged as the hide
Of the grown alligator.
A young alligator squirmed on his naked knees
While he muttered its lesson.

That was strong medicine. Over the old man's eyes
    Drooped the holy beloved crest of the swan-plumes;
Otter-skin straps cut under his arms
From the breastplate of conch-shells.
Fawn-trotters fell from his boot-tops; the white beloved
    mantle
Lined with raw scarlet, hung on the gum-tree, along with
    the ocelot quiver
    And locust-wood bow.
He had fasted, drinking the dark button snake-root. He
    shuddered,
Calling the secret name, the name of the Manneyto,
Y-O-He,
Never known by the people.

On the infant saurian, long-lived, ruled into patterns, his
   hands
Moved, taking the shape of a sharp-curved arrow;
He spoke, teaching its lesson, calling its name;
"Nanneb-Chunchaba,
Fish-like-a-Mountain,
Remember!

"By the day-sun and the night-sun,
By the new beloved fire of the corn-feast;
By the Arrow of Lightning, that came from the storm,
From the Spirit of Fire to the ancient chief of the
   Yemassee—
Totem of Yemassee!
Let our voice be remembered.

"We go from the hunting-grounds of our fathers,
The lands that we took, fighting north through the man-
   eating Westoes,
Fall from our hands.
In the hills of our dead, in the powdering flesh that
   conceived us,
Shall the white man plant corn.

"The trails where we fought with the fierce Tuscarora
Will call us in vain;
No pictures of skillful canoemen will green Isundiga paint
   clear in his waters.
We shall be cut from the land as the medicine-man cuts
   the totem
From the arm of the outcast.

"*From the sky they cannot cut our totem!*

"My name too shall vanish.
When the drums and the music for three days are silent
And men praise me under the peach-trees,
My over-wise spirit

Shall root itself here, as the oak-tree takes hold.
Who will wait for me? Which of the spirits
That have made of my body a lodge, that have twisted
    my sinews
As women twist withes for their baskets, will claim
    habitation,
That have spoken their wisdom
Out of my mouth?
I shall hide from them all, as the war-chiefs
Cover their lives with the tree-tops,
Leaving them safe when they go on the war-path.
I shall sleep in this place.

"In the new days,
The days when our voice shall be silent,
Speak for the Yemassee!
Nanneb-Chunchaba, you, little Fish-like-a-Mountain,
Shout through the forest the terrible war-cry of Yemassee!

"*Sangarrah!* . . . *Sangarrah-me!* . . . *Sangarrah-me!*
Shout! I shall hear you!
Sangarrah! . . ."

For two hundred years—
Will, without inflexion—
The bull alligator
Roars from the swamp
In the Spring.

THE YEMASSEE LANDS

I

In the Yemassee Lands
Peace-belts unwind in the Spring on the banks of Savannah;
Flowers like wampum weave in the grass
Reiterate beads of pink-orange, of clouded white, of
    pale, shimmerless ochre,
Mile after mile.

II

Round the curve of the river,
Meshed by conniving impatient shoots of the gum tree,
Streamers of silver dart, muffled lapping of paddles.
Always, just round the turning, the stealthy canoe
    with its naked upstanding warrior
Comes . . . for the wild-fowl rise in a hurtling of
    startled feathers;
Never comes into sight.

III

In the Yemassee Lands
Cypress roots, at the edge of the swamp, roughly
    fluted, age-wrinkled,
Have budded their rufous knobs like dim and reptilian eyes,
That watch.
Orchids, liquid gold, bend from cylindrical sheaths
Under a phantom moccasined tread.
Gossamer webs, barring the overgrown way through
    the woods,
Shudder but do not break, betraying the passage
Of footsteps gone by.

IV

In the undulant mist of the sunsets of summer
Slim pines stand with scarlet and quivering outlines—

Initiate boys whose whipped young blood leaps up
Now, the first time, to the war-path.
Shadows of red, shadows of bronze and of copper
Disengage from the wood-growth;
Cowering, melting, lost, reappearing,
One after one, the long, lithe, menacing war-line
Loops through the stems.
Light cups the crouching knees,
Splinters on polished shoulders,
Ravels in towering head-plumes.

V

In the Yemassee Lands
When with blowing of wood-smoke and throbbing
   of hidden drums
Indian Summer fashions its spell,
Trembling falls on the air.
Wild things flatten themselves in the jeopardy of the
   shade.
Out of the snarling keen-toothed vines
Berries wink with the cunning obsidian gleam
Of the arrow-head, and deep in the shuddering fern
The rattlesnake coils his pattern of war.
Silence, inimical, lurks in the dark:
Softly on buckskinned soles, halting a step behind,
Something follows and waits . . .
And will not be appeased.

VI

But when Autumn unleashes the winds
And storm treads the lowlands,
Trees, like a panic of horses galloping over the sky-line,
(Charging of chestnut and roan and bay,
Tossing their frantic forelocks)
Flee from the rush
Of invisible hunters.

VII

Stars in the coppery afterglow of the sundown
Hang like strings of teeth on the savage breast of a warrior;
Water-willows trail in the shadowy depths of Savannah,
Draggle like scalps from the war-belt;
And the night-wind sings overhead
Like arrows on deadly sendings,
In the Yemassee Lands.

VIII

Gray through young leaves blows the smoke from the
    ancient fires;
The thud of the young men's dances troubles the earth.
Shadows from ambushed boughs
Reach with a plucking hand for the hair.
The lightning-set pine far away blazes with
    hideous cracklings,
Remembering the long black tresses of captive
    squaws
Tied to the death-pyre.

IX

After two hundred years
Has the forest forgotten?
Always the trees are aware
(Significant, perilous, shaken with whispers of dread
    and of welcome)
Of the passage of urgent feet.
Violent shoots strain up to the air and the sunshine
Of cut-over land;
Leaves crowd over the barrows of last year's skeleton
    leaves.
Ever and ever again
The Red Man comes back to his own
In the Yemassee Lands.

THE GONG

Love hums in your veins with the deep and heartening sound
Of a temple gong—
The gong of Dai Nippon
That fused into perfect, fastidious harmony
When a girl had flung into the quag of its white-hot metal
Her rhythm of passionate life.

In the dead hours of the day
When men doubt themselves,
When the acrid sunlight appraises them and finds them
    without due significance,
You touch for your own reassurance
The gong!
And its soft-toned thunder, musical, purple, true as earth's
    center—
Dignity, power, conviction—
Imposes its harmony:
One may believe in oneself without insulting intelligence,
Life may be full of distinction, of ordered beauty—and
    magic—
And you are the master!

The rhythm of blood and of spirit run true.
When has she failed you?
When withheld immolation
In the fiery quicksand?

TIDEWATER

I

COASTS

Were the burned sands of Aeaea—
Circe's—stranger than yours,
Wadmalaw?
Myrtles squat beastlike, each crouching inland,
Sand for a spell on their faces.

Is Samos more white
Than the beaches of Kiawah?
Are the knightly spirits of Rhodes more
    fiercely splendid
Than phantoms of Indian warriors?
Their lances more terrible
Than points of palmetto and yucca
Crossed like a sword-dance
On Edisto?
Their towers more arrogant
Than the belfries of thick white bell-flowers
Carved on the air?

Is Marathon richlier echoed
With voices of youthful heroes
Than the swamps of Santée?
When the bloom runs over the moss
In a lost gray glory of tarnished silver,
    of shadowy pearl,
Riders furrow the night—
Marion, Marion's men,
Pass in a voiceless tumult,
Pass like the smoke from a torch,
With dark, unextinguished eyes.

These are the coasts, the haunted coasts and
    the islands
Of Carolina.

II

HARBOR WATER

All through the night I can hear the sound of dancers,
Soft-padding hoofs, and the lipping of the water,
The water, the water patting juba . . .

> *Juba! Juba!*
> *Juba lef' an' juba right,*
> *Juba dance on a moonshine night—*
> *Juba!*

Knobbly palmetto posts,
Matted trunks of sea-gods,
Hairier than monkeys, rise from the water—
The pulpy, the oily-burnished water.

Soft rocking feet of the dancers sway about them,
Long-swelling ripples with their crisp inhibitions,
Filed golden streaks like the pointed feet of dancers,
Pull of the tide, and the netted flopping motion
Of the water, the music-woven, oily-damasked water,
Water patting juba . . .

> *Juba! Juba!*
> *Juba lef' an' juba right,*
> *Juba dance on a moonshine night—*
> *Juba!*

III

DEW

The new morning light is a primitive,
A painter of faintly-filled outlines,
    A singer of folk-songs.

The dew-flattened vines by my window
Are all of one innocent green.

Nothing so young as that green—
An outline cut by a child
     From a soft new blotter.

But when the light grows,
They suck up a pert chiaroscuro,
Gold meretricious knowing high-lights,
     Hopelessly clever.

     Their poems
     Dry in the sun.

IV

WHITE AZALEAS IN MAGNOLIA GARDENS

Your images in water! Sea-shell grays
And iridescence; like the endless spawn
Of pale sea-jellies on a moonless night—
A milky way that glamors out of sight—
Something of sea and something of the sky.
Drawn from the earth as blossoming dreams are drawn,
Most strange are you in this, that dreams alight and fly,
But you dream on all your translucent days.

Sweeps of divinest nothingness, abyss
Of beauty, you are the stirred subconscious place
Of flowers, you are the rathe and virgin mood
Of young azaleas.
          Where heaped branches brood
Like bathers, water-girdled to the hips,
Like Undines, every blossom turns her face
Groping above the water, with her parted, winged,
     insatiable lips,
Each for her soul and its white mysteries.

LILL' ANGELS

Mammy rocks the baby
  In the wallflower-colored gloom,
All the floor rocks with her
  And the slumber of the room.
Like the broad, unceasing trade-wind,
  Like the rivers underground,
Rolls the universal rhythm
  And the rich primeval sound:
    All de lill' angels,
    All de baby's angels,
      Swingin' on de tree;
    Forty-one lill' angel,
    Fifty-two lill' angel,
    Sixty-fo' lill' angel,
      Sebbenty-t'ree . . .
In the glory of the sundown
  Of the wallflower-colored skies,
I can see her vast Assumption
  In a cloud of cherubs' eyes.
With their gold-persimmon haloes,
  Where the ripest sunlight falls
And the cherub-tree's espaliered
  On the winking crystal walls—
    Little yaller angels,
    Piccaninny angels,
      Chuckle on the tree.
    Forty-one lill' angel,
    Fifty-two lill' angel,
    Sixty-fo' lill' angel,
      Sebbenty-t'ree . . .

FIRST LOVE

I

I am the whispering doorway, I am the beckoning threshold,
Calling the passer-by.
I am all welcome!

I am what comes to me, not what goes out.
I am not in my hands nor my feet nor the long wings of my
    thoughts:
I am in answers.

I lie on my bed and my spirit frequents hilltops;
My hands thread fingers with pine-fans;
The dappled pattern of moonlight
Leaps after me like a tree-cat.
The trumpet-vine chatters with voices of infant parrots;
Like great orbs of owls the night flowers open their eyes.
If I say, All is One, seven times over,
I shall believe it.

II

I have made me an answer.
I have made me a man to love.
The willow tree grows in the grass near to my window—
Frighteningly near at night—
It rounded its garlands of leaves curved as an empty bell
Till I set you under its arches, its desolate aching spaces
Like music,
Dark and reverberant music of bell notes.

III

The wind shakes the branch like the garlanded shaft of
    a spear
Dreaming of lions.
Wait but a little. Oh, do not answer.

Comfort me first with your silence, the smart of your
    deprivation
Holding its breath.
        My thoughts are but air-plants, groping for
        footholds, lost in your tree,
Prehensile, with nails, with soft hooks, fingering their
    points of vantage—
No!
        My thoughts are like strong-muscled runners, fleeing
        before you,
Burning my face with sparks from their back-blown
    torches.

IV

Is it the wind or your singing?
Sparks of white sea-spray burned on my mouth, and the
    music
Rolled like the wheels of young porpoises, over and over,
Playing with storms.
I was scattered like spray, rainbowed spray on the arches
    of cataracts
In the rainbow music of cataracts . . .
Letting me go, after new births and new centuries
Dropping me back into the finite forgotten body.

V

I cannot remember you
After you go.
I hold you as the poplar holds the storm—
Beautiful tumult!
Covering the glint of its leaves
With abashed white eyelids.

THE PIRATES

The garden of Garret Vanselvin
Swam in the golden spray of October.
The Mexican rose, like a sun-dial,
In tremulous upstaring blossoms
Told off the day:—
Gemmules, white for the dawn; flushing with desperate
  hope in the noon;
And drawn into cowering balls of disastrous red—
Thrown-away red—with the sundown.
Into the wide-set windows
Catspaws of south-flavored wind laughed from the harbor,
Where the town, like a giant child, sat on the knees of the
  islands
And played with a lapful
Of silvery ships.

Did they watch it, day after day—
The pirates—
The doomed gold arcs of their hours slip through the
  sun-dial tree?

In the house-place of Garret Vanselvin—
Charles Town, in the province of South Carolina,
Seventeen-hundred-eighteen—
They were trying the pirates;
Men of Stede Bonnet's, shipmates of Vaughn and of
  Blackbeard;
Noisome things of the sea, vicious with spines, smeared
  with abhorrent blood.
They had scooped them a netful and flung it into a corner.
This vile *frutto di mare.*

The pearly swell and the color of coral and amber drained
  out of them,
Flaccid and lax they lay,
Hardly with wills to answer, only waiting the outcome,

47

The gasp in this cursed, foreign air,
The last alien strangle . . .

What did they dream of day after day, the trammeled
    sea-creatures?
It all must have tasted of dreams.
Dry waves and billows of sound, climbing, discharging
    above them;
Voices of lawyers, sleek, desiccate, deadly.
All of eleven judges.
Chief Justice, black-robed, wigged and appurtenanced,
    just as in England.
Goose-Creek gentry the rest, well-born planters come from
    Barbadoes;
Gentlemen laced and red-coated, men of the crack troop
    of horse
Coloneled by Logan.
A shifting of juries.
And all of them, gentle and simple, cut to the quick of
    their pride and their pockets
When the seemly and gravid rice-ships, matronly moving
    out of the harbor,
Plumped in the arms of fell and insolent sea-thieves
Skulking outside.
Wait!
Chief Justice Nicholas Trott, Judge of the Court of
    Vice-Admiralty,
He it is, speaking.
Will he remember?—

Governor once of Providence in the Bahamas,
Not unreputed as over-friendly to rovers,
Not unrebuked for their fellowship.
For the sake of old days, will he . . .
Wait!

His voice! Those are the melting, significant accents
That won on their lordships in London, that pull at the
    eyelids

Of lattice-bred women. (Their women live here behind
  windows and iron-tusked walls.
You passed them—the narrow, still streets, ambushed with
  eyes—you two who bore Blackbeard's message,
Laying their high-stomached Province under his contribution.—
Ay, but that flicked them!)
Hearken!

And first he lifts from your shoulder the cover of common
  humanity.
Men? You are not men. You are *hostes humani generis*,
Enemies of all mankind. Neither faith, nay, nor oath need
  be kept with you.
You were formerly ousted of clergy.
Now the law grants you this comfort; and, with a smooth
  lovingkindness
Equal to that of the law, he trusts you will profit.
But—he may allow you no counsel.

He is telling you further
That the God of the land made the ocean,
  (He swivels the Scriptures about like a gun, texts spitting
  for grapeshot);
That he parceled it out and placed it under the thumbs of
  Kings and of lawyers.
(O ye fowls of the air, ye wild winds, ye waterspouts,
Praise ye the Lord!)
And against all these three, God, King and lawyers, have
  you offended.

And the witnesses now.
Will they humor the gentry, tickle their notion of pirates'
  ways,
Got from old chap-books, old songs of the Barbary Coast?
Pshaw! This is tame, this has no tang!
No decks swashing in blood? No one walking the plank?
You, James Killing, mate of the ravished sloop, *Francis,*
Did they not cut you down?—Nay, and their captain, he
  that's escaped, Major Bonnet,

49

Was civil, uncommon civil.—Cutlasses drawn?—Why,
    yes . . .
To cut down the pineapple-nets over the captain's lockers.
Asked me to join in a health in rum punch to the King—
    over the water;
Asked why I looked so melancholy. Told them I looked
    as well as I could.
Sang two-three glees . . . asked me to join'em a-pirating.
And now they are questioning you.
How came you such monsters, outlaws?
Not by your wills? Forced to that way of life? Why did
    you join then?
How should one tell this Judge, in his awful and spiteful
    majesty,
His sinister magpie dress,—
"Man—or, my lord—or your honor—had you been left
    on a Maroon shore,
With the sea in front and behind you a present death—
    Indians howling at night,
Or worser than Indians, made out of night, broke loose
    from hell—
Just for the smell of a ship and the jog of a shipmate's
    elbow
You'd have turned pirate too!"
God! How mouth it
To his honor, a Lord Chief Justice?

What does it profit to listen
To the long, long, day-long drone,
While the sun spills gold through the Mexican rose-tree?
Better to listen instead
To the winding importunate wind, blowing up from
    palm-tasseled Barbadoes;
Wind that damasks the water, silky wind in the sails
When, like an overripe fruit, rolled in the quickening wash,
The ship is tugging at anchor.
Wind like the hair of girls, so soft, so perfumed and
    resilient,

Tangling the memory now . . .

But here, swelled with importance,
Assistant-Judge Thomas Hepworth, dangerous, droll as
    a pincushion-fish, altercative,
Turns to the jury.
Shall the Carolinas be ruined as one hears that Jamaica
    is ruined?
Are not our rice-ships seized at our very gates?
Is not the incredible true? In our own walled town what
    disturbance, what rioting,
What threatenings to burn it—burn Charles Town—burn
    it about our ears!
And all with design
To rescue these pestilent pirates.
Only too well have arts and practice effected
The flight of Stede Bonnet. Certain are favorable toward
    him,
Citing his gentle blood, his fortune, his education—
Enhancements these of his crimes.
An example then, gentlemen all, a substantial and speedy
    example:
The times demand it!

And the trial clicks to the verdict.

No record remains
In the ancient records of Charles Town,
No scribble, no note—
Only the outraged, discretionless speech of his judgeship,
Forwarded straight to London, from his Majesty's Court
    of Vice-Admiralty,
Witnesses yet
To the people's love for the pirates.

They threw doubloons on the counters
Of honest taverns fringing the wharves.
It was Fair-day in Charles Town harbor,

Silks to be bought good cheap, spices and loaves of
  blue-coated sugar,
When the sunburned traffickers landed.
Trinkets they fetched and wines . . .
Ah, but richer and fiercer,
Surely they brought Romance!
(Do you notice that burly man, his scared eyes watching
  the captives
As men watch plague-struck comrades?
Do you mark that girl, twisting, with hunted glances,
Her apron-tail in her teeth?)
They brought in their stained red scarves aromas of
  dangerous rapture
That comfort men who live by the sea and resist its
  challenge,—
Romance that lifted the blurred, resentful drab of their
  days
As sunrise opals the sea-mist.

As the shop of a Greek near the wharves
Where the quick white sailors cluster like sea-gulls
Over his tubs of grapes, his ropy netting of melons,
I shall stop, I shall buy a pineapple,
Heavy with tropic flavors.
I shall go to the White Point gardens, as near as may be
To the place where we hanged the pirates—
We Carolinians—
Where the gun from Granville Bastion
Ripped the sky with the sunrise;
And the merciful quicksand took them,—
Twisted, discolored sea-things.

I shall study my pineapple,
Its desperate-clinging points . . .
As a man might cling to life with his finger-nails and his
  toe-nails

When the breath is squeezed in his throat!
As one lays flowers on a grave
I shall toss it over the sea-wall.

Because you laughed when you ravished the *Francis;*
Because you drank to your fallen King—over the water;
But most because they once loved you,
The humble, whose very life is in some sort a piracy,
Marauding the sun and air from the well-found and solid
    citizen;
Because they fought for your lives—
May your quicksand, O pirates,
Be soft as the arms of a girl,
May your sleep be forever
And pleasant with dreams of sea-changes,

Interpreters of the sea!

"OF GARDENS"

My lord Saint Albans, my lord Verulam,
Observes his garden; in his subtile hand
The latest blooming of his Essayes, new enlarged.
As one should verify his classical citations,
His Virgil or his Metamorphoses,
He comes to measure with the rich original
His copy, clipped but yet luxuriant,
"Of Gardens,"
And finds it like enough.

Not with his fabled pleasance for a Prince,
With sculptured wall-springs and their fine avoidances,
Cloisters and Covert Alleys;
But with the place his taste for temperate splendors
Had fashioned. He was in the mellow season,
Pulchrorum Autumnus pulcher;
Spring he distrusted, being no longer young,
Nor ever prone to wanton ebulliency;
"For no *Youth* can be comely, but by Pardon,"
So had he written. Once he could pardon Spring,
And scant no season, hanging impartially
His garlands on the year. Yes, even after
His Fall had suffered blight.
But these last months—
He wondered should the tenuous, perfumed trumpets
Of Spring's young harbingers rouse him another time.

"Crocus Vernus, both the Yellow and the Gray;
Prime-Roses; Anemones; The Early Tulippa;
Hyacinthus Orientalis;
Chamairis."

He turned to gardens as men turn to toys
When too much shattered by reality.
He had good precedent.
After His labor with the dreadful, untried engines

Of light and land and sea, the unaccountable machines
Of birds and beasts and fishes, quick with a little life,
Running to play with it to unguessed ends,
The Almighty turned to toys
And planted Him a garden.
Why, so could he, having all substances
God had to work with,
Heavens and earth, the atoms and the void,
As saith Democritus.
He could proceed from the known to the unknown,
From seeds to towering trees, from single to frilled corollas,
Flowers as paynim as the Alcoran;
And learn, as God discerned
When forms reared up between his molding palms,
Form is the thing itself.

A forward season: here are April's forms betimes:

"The Couslip; Flower-Delices, & Lilies of all Natures;
Rose-mary Flowers; The Tulippa; The Double Piony;
The Pale Daffadill; The French Honny-Suckle;
The Cherry-Tree in Blossome;
The Dammasin, and Plum-Trees in Blossome;
The White-Thorne in Leafe;
The Lelacke Tree."

One well might be
A paltry god in gardens, one might cut
Planets in Welts and Satellites of Juniper,
Call constellations of golden apricots
From out of nothing, Galaxies of crab-apples,
And grovelling worlds of melons
Where plums fell thick as shooting stars in midsummer.
One showed a lovingkindness to his creatures,
Thinning rank flowers lest virtuous fruit-trees be deprived.
And one took gifts from fruit-trees without blame.

"In *August,* come Plummes of all sorts in Fruit;
Peares; Apricockes; Berberries; Filberds;

55

Muske-Melons; Monks Hoods, of all colours. In *September,*
Come Grapes; Apples; Poppies of all colours;
Peaches; Melo-Cotones; Nectarines; Cornelians;
Wardens; Quinces."

Strange, as all learning teaches, that this world
Should be the same eternally, rock should be indurate rock
And man be man, unchanged since Adam's Eden,
When all things change in gardens;
Fountains must flow or harbor noisome frogs,
And breath of flowers grows stale within the hand
And must, like music, be continually reborn.
"There is no Excellent *Beauty* that hath not some
     Strangenesse";
You found it so.
And what more strange than beauty in the making;
More strange, confusing Nature, than the avian fashion
Of peaches, fledglings in their leafy nests;
More strange than herbs
That prosper, smilling sweetly, trodden on?
     "Burnet, Wilde-Time, and Water-Mints."
These three.

It was late Fall with him. Deciduous honors had abandoned
     him,
Men's fairy-gold opinions.
Where all was strange, at early candle-lighting
Who might not walk through pleachèd alley-ways?
A fellow-husbandman?
They had companioned to create a beauty,
Using each other's tools, smiling the dim guild-smile, the
     craftsman's smile,
When ventures flourished.
Will God be less abounding than a garden?
If he would save his soul, it must be done
As he had bidden painters limn a face,
Not by the rules,
But by a sort of outlaw, fine Felicity.

Or, it may be,
One needs small hope of God,
And comes to gardens as Lazarus blocked the threshold
Of that great lord, waiting that pointed shadows
Of branches, like the healing tongues of dogs,
Might lick his sores.

His choice must be:

"Such Things, as are Greene all Winter:
Holly; Ivy; Bayes; Iuniper; Cipresse Trees."

His bays were blown upon. Only the ivy
That tolerantly comforts old men's graves,
Or cypress, Death's tried ancient, bearer of his colors,
For him.
(He died next April.)

My lord Saint Albans, my lord Verulam,
Considers gardens.

EVOLUTION

What night so disarmed, so confiding as this night?
The garnered heat of the day
Puffs through the weeds.
The channels of roots are disturbed and wrung with new
 voices.
Tree branches are fruited with stars and the sky-spaces
 rustle with leaves.
Evocative smells, plaited together with creepers, rush past.
Cruising with night-moths
Petals tear themselves loose from the stems.
With delicate animal wickerings
Bamboos charge, wild as a flight of young antelope.

The senses mingle their borders,
Dove-tail.
Distant water sprays into coolness,
Rasping of boughs troubles the skin, intimate as a touch.
Everything reaches out after some untried encounter;
And the unguarded spirit,
Like earth that would be a plant, like a crowded leaf
That would net its veins over the fans of a butterfly,
Strains at the moorings
Of a body that holds it
Away from some beckoning skyline!

THE HUMMING-BIRD

The sundial makes no sign
At the point of the August noon.
The sky is of ancient tin,
And the ring of the mountains diffused and unmade
(One always remembers them).
On the twisted dark of the hemlock hedge
Rain, like a line of shivering violin-bows
Hissing together, poised on the last turgescent swell,
Batters the flowers.
Under the trumpet-vine arbor,
Clear, precise as an Audubon print,
     The air is of melted glass,
     Solid, filling interstices
Of leaves that are spaced on the spines
     Like a pattern ground into glass;
     Dead, as though dull red glass were poured into
  the mouth,
Choking the breath, molding itself into the creases of
  soft red tissues.

And a humming-bird darts head first,
Splitting the air, keen as a spurt of fire shot from the
  blow-pipe,
Cracking a star of rays; dives like a flash of fire,
Forked tail lancing the air, into the immobile trumpet;
Stands on the air, wings like a triple shadow
Whizzing around him.

Shadows thrown on the midnight streets by a snow-flecked
  arc-light,
Shadows like sword-play,
Splinters and spines from a thousand dreams
Whizz from his wings!

SPRING MOSS

These are the fringes of long-tailed birds
That sleep in Death's aviaries.
These
Are the strings of the harps that are borne before
His singers of pedigrees;
Echoing silvery names that are loud no more,
And ermined heraldic words.

These are the jasmines, the white white roses, the eglantines
That garland with tiers of their indolent curves
Death's balladines.
And these, when his torturers handle the curdling flesh
Of dreams, these are the fine-drawn nerves,
Hung in a gasping tangle, a squirming and quicksilver
  mesh.

This is the conquering beauty of Death, sardonic, his
  arrogant play;
Cat's-cradles of ruin he hangs on the tight-clenched cones
  of the pines,
In the teeth of the day.

THE OLD MAN

Do they ever grow really old,
Do they cease to believe in miracles?

He sits in the Park,
His buttonhole blooms unconcerned, a bud in the crack
    of a ruin;
His fine, gathered fingers curl upward:
He is holding hands with the sun.

Like a girl's shadow
The furtive smell of the Spring runs over his face.

"She would come like that,
A little abashed, a little defiant . . ."
He fondles the past in his palms with the alchemical sun.
The past?
"She will come . . ."
The future is coming!

THE JESUIT MISSIONARIES

Like soldiers they took their orders,
Marching to certain glory.
And like soldiers they wrote
From the Front back to Headquarters;
No compromise to flatter a difficult public,
But cogent reports to their General,
Stark awful reality.

Scourged, bitten with fire,
Battling with beasts, with fever, with a novel and strange
    demonology;
In the face of long and fastidious torture,
They saved, like feathery, Spring-leaved brands plucked
    from the burning,
The souls of red children.

They were nowise concerned whether the climate
Might pamper a wife, what education
Might nourish her offspring.
Traveling light, going alone and farthest,
They followed the Spirit.
Others have followed them—
Makers of books and of records
Turning to splendid names:
Brébeuf, Daniel, Raymbault,
Jogues, first light to the Mohawk.
There is the fruitful witness—
"Relations." "Relations." "Jesuit Relations."
The foot-notes rise up, call them blessèd—
Fathers of American History!

ON *A SUN-DIAL*

Follow the Sun as I   : his Favour keep
Nor fear the Night that cometh : Sweet is Sleep

INTERVALS

I shall make offering in a new basket of marsh-grass
Curved like a conch-shell, sharp with salt echoes,
Two long handles like looped arms.
Untamed things shall I bring to the god of gardens,
Plum-blossom, sweet-olive and thyme,
Tang of small figs, gone wild in deserted gardens,
Most subtle of trees as the serpent is subtlest of beasts,
Slouched on the heat-soaked walls . . .
I shall lay them under the weary, appraising eyes,
The cynical musical fingers
That rest on the goat-thighs.
Let me give him, O Pan,
All in the way of love—
The new keen edge of difference,
The wonder of being together,
And the wild taste of immemorial marsh-grass.
But in the intervals,
When the lover is gone and only the comrade remains,
Pan, have mercy!
Teach me to talk like a man!

SALVAGE

Three things in my house are my own.
Not the dark pictures whose blood runs in my veins,
Nor the vines that I trained round the windows,
Nor even the books.
But the curve of a shabby armchair that molded
   itself on your body,
And the echoes of songs that you sang,
And the square of sun
That comes as it came, first in the morning,
When you had opened the window.

POE'S MOTHER

It's something to be born at sea, as I
Was born. Earth fails to get full clutch on you.
You keep a certain cleanliness of depths—
Soul, self-respect, you call it what you like.
There's evil in the sea, but cleaner evil,
Chasms of swallowing ultramarine, cold, cold,
Where pulsing moons and devil-fish like stars
May eat you, but crystal-blooded, without passion.
The ocean always keeps about your neck
One tentacle, sucks gently at your veins
Until you yield and lapse to him once more.
I love such crazy fancies, early mornings,
When nothing's very real. The babies sleeping
Safe islanded in small worlds of their own;
And two good hours before the wench comes in
With tea (her tea *tastes* surly), and the *Courier;*
The sea-breeze, slitting through the broken shutter,
Magnolias, too far off to sicken one,
Across the balcony where, strung with vines,
The metal twists a lyre! Eddie saw it—
That child sees everything. This is the hour
I love, the unrealest hour of all the day,
When beauty's more than stage-plays, when ill-will
And debts and duns, and even the superbities
Of that damned Beaumont woman (not a chance
Of any decent part with her), and even—
And even David—O God, where is he now?—
Forsake me like a tide that's going out.
My cough itself grows better in this air;
Mild, vivid Charleston April, lax and salty
As gusts from sea-flowers. Lying half-alive
I watch the sky grow saffron, bluish-pink,
Like colored drawings travelers bring from Venice
Or pearl-crimped shells from Caribbean islands.
For these two hours I can forgive the world,
Forgive myself. Why, when my mind needs comfort

Must it flow always to that same old season
Two years ago, as though that promised me
Some unsuspected, some—*foreboding* good—
Good prismed with darkness? *Yes.* We played in Boston
Together. Eddie came. I hardly rested.
Oh, gentles, think that I played Juliet!
Would you believe it? Could you fancy it?

Juliet, the girl whom everybody loves.
Why has the world conspired to clothe its dream
Of utter beauty in a velvet pall,
With pallid velvet tapers, head and feet,
In Capulet's monument? Perhaps to claim
That beauty is real, the flaws are accidents.
Or, it may be, since this world must be damned,
A foredoomed planet (that's what Beaumont tells me),
To stand (I love that) on the defiant thesis
That death itself can be adorable.

Two years ago I never had such thoughts.
It seemed quite natural the world should love us—
Juliet was I and I was Juliet,
Not dead but dreaming, living, to bring forth life.
(If ever there was a love-child it was Eddie).
We quarreled and we hated but, merciful heaven,
What difference does that make when people love
Each other? Yes, and Juliet too—who knows,
Who knows that she was not a rose in bud
As well?

       Oh, elegant and poetic way
To put the ugliest miracle in life!
Don't let me think of that—that's waiting for me!
Ungainliness and sickness, sickness, anguish,
And David gone, and grinding weariness
Of making both ends meet. Let me get the good
Of these two unreal hours. Let me be quiet.
The only bearable things in life are dreams.

A queer man, that man Beaumont, brittle, white
As chalk without his make-up, with an ear
Cocked over his shoulder, listening, so you'd say,
For that strange slow disease that's killing him.
Always implying, surmising love to me—
Well, heaven knows, he must be sick enough
Of second fiddle to his Olympian missus,
New-lighted, like a goddess from her car,
From Covent Garden. Most, he slinks aside,
A well-kicked dog, to work on plays no playhouse
Will risk. I dropped a friendly word one day.
He smiled. "Don't pity me, my lovely Betsey,
Blood of its martyrs is the seed of art . . .
Has it occurred to you that Something throws
Our moods at us, our churning, troubled backgrounds,
As stage mechanics throw their rays and shadows,
To work, not good to us, but His effects?"
I asked, "Do you mean God?" He laughed this time.
And I: "If trouble's all the gifts it takes
Someday I'll try my hand at plays myself."
"Women write plays? God gave them His first law
Of self-expression, never gave a second:
'Ladies, I beg you'll have the condescension—
Forgive my taste—to increase and multiply!' "
With such a grand Lord Orville kind of bow,
I had to laugh, though I was angry too.

Beaumont, the least attaching sort of man,
Why must he draw me? He takes me from myself?
His bitterness is whole as other's passion
And modulates his love, as wind and water
Enrich each other in a stormy picture.
Women he scorns, they barely save themselves
By being mothers. Once, he said, some poet
Proclaimed the sea the chariot of nature.
Was I, sea-born, meant only for the bringer,
The chariot of children? Will's no care,
All day he's with the young ones of the house,
But this strange other baby—

They talk of changelings,
Born with old memories. No child should live
The moods—they can't be thoughts—behind his eyes;
Crushed mulberry shadows washed around the lids.
I almost could believe God threw His shadows
Across my skies and worked my cloudy ferment
To shape this child.

He's born of Juliet's body!

It isn't me he wants, it's only love,
To feel himself alive in someone else.
He holds me off even while he clings to me,
His fingers on my mouth: "Sing, sing—not talk!"
What will become of him? I know, I know
The child's *alone!*

What will become of them? Two helpless children
And one more coming.—I mustn't think of that!
I mustn't cry. I'll wake them. Where's the paper,
The yesterday's, the slattern wench forgot?
Behind the bureau. Can I reach it? There.
Of course there's nothing but the bare announcement
Of our next play. The perfect Charleston manner,
To look with distant, not unfriendly eyes
On those quaint animals, the player-folk,
But scarcely serve them with the gentry's breakfast;
No puffs nor praises, though there have been pleas
That gentlemen who cluster in the wings
Should go, nor discommode the actresses.
Here's what I'm looking for. *"The Winter's Tale."*
(I'm Mopsa). "Mrs. Beaumont's Benefit."
When will that woman go and let me play
More than a maid, a Mog, a mountebank?
Before she came they gave me *Lady Teazle,
Lydia.*

Oh God, I once was Juliet!
Don't think of that! What else? A hundred boxes
Of Cheese, true Paté-Grasse. And, Lor', I wish
Some friend remembered me! *Lines to a Chimney Sweeper.*
The Lottery for the Presbyterian Church,
To "raise an edifice to the most HIGH."
Some likely negro wenches to be hired.
I wish I had one. I'd dress her to the life
As Beaumont-Roxalana in *The Sultan.*
Oh look! At Mrs. Henry's, Elliot Street,
Brought by the brig *Eliz,* straight from London,
Rosettes and Silver Bandoes, Jaconet,
Gauze, Lawns and Tiffany, and Garden fans
With sticks of ivory, and Brunswick Slippers.
White Brunswick Slippers! Mine are over-run
And both the buckles tarnished. Jaconet,
So sweet for tunics with a Highland ribbon
On little boys. Oh Lord, oh Lord—

                              That's me!
I'll cry as hard as that for anything:
My cough, a part, David, my soul's salvation,
Or all the sorrows of this wicked world,
As for a length of gauze! That's Betsey Arnold.
I know how those Aeolean things must feel
They rig on our piazza. Any breath
Will set me off. Oh hush, you idiot fool!
You couldn't tell to save your precious neck
Which one you're crying for. Most like the slippers,
With heels to challenge feathers in your hair
Which is the lightest; so that Beaumont's eyes
May follow you with human moisture in them.
What would it be to love a man like that,
A man who works, who's bitter-true and genuine
As men are only in romantic plays?
As real as unreality.

We hate
His wife with perfect and voluptuous hatred . . .
But what's the good? He wouldn't be the end.
I'd hanker after some archangel next,
Riding his fiery charger through the sunset.
All, all my life I've wanted the next highest
To feel myself dragged back—the silver chains
Of seas, or jet-black chains of this vile earth!
How many, many things one mustn't think of!
A ravening horde of thoughts that long to stamp
Above my pitiful drift-fire, put it out—

There now, I've waked him!
                    No, he mustn't cry!
Don't cry, my little, little, darling lamb!
His mother'll wrap him in the counterpane,
The pretty white-and-purple patchwork thing,
And rock him on the balcony. She'll sing
Of cities in the water, just like this,
And flowers that bloom when everyone's asleep;
And he shall watch the steeples, and the point
Of that long heaving island, and the sunrise
That catches every color on the marsh.
She'll make the whole world pretty for him! Yes—
We'll sing—not talk . . . we'll sing . . .

PART TWO

Other Poems

ALL HALLOWS

He told me, "I went to a church."
(For a whisper, a touch, a shred of awareness?)
"The worthy young rector, (hurried, a trifle),
Spoke of the higher life,
Of the robust searching of spirit
Before one 'belonged.'
One felt that his wife had admonished him
That an overdone dinner was an abomination before the
      Lord,
And her mother was exigent.

"And out of the dark came floating
The dense, agonizing Cathedral
Down below the Gulf,
The music that pumped currents of magic
Into your nerves,
The high, proud archangel-windows, tranquil in war-harness.
Over the altar, like a straight light in your eyes,
The cross made you helpless.
The strange old priest,
Far-off as some rubbing from a pale-bronze tomb,
(Gentle, tortured lines in his face
Of ancient renunciations),
Said, as one having authority,
Comforting as sleep comforts,
(While the long black veils lifted like twilight leaves),
'My children, to-day our dead come back to us.'

"His voice made a nest for them,
The shy, reluctant ones;
They would hardly have known the difference."

(1921)

75

THE DAMP GARDEN

Lizards grow on my balcony vines, and drop like long beans.
There are snails with crimped borders,
Sea-creature borders, pearly and hostile.
They have lost their sea echoes. . . . Listen!

Under my balcony men swarmed with the night.
Guitars sang . . "Ah! . . . Senorita,
You are too beauitful . . . it is a sin!"
Their songs, their eyes like unhappy glowworms,
Were all just the same.
Now—there are only whispers all over the garden,
Everywhere are the whispers.
And the soft, wet hands of the bald-headed, watchful old
        Doctor
Leave on my wrists silvery streaks like thin bracelets,—
Or is it the snails?

Ghosts do not come any more. It is terribly sinister being
        without them.
Worse must have scared them away.
I shall climb by the vines up the wall, by the hungry spikes
        in the vines.
I shall ask of the first passer-by:
"Senor, for the love of God's Mother, whose is this terrible
        garden?
And who is this woman?"

(*1923*)

76

FEAR

I am not afraid of fire,
Nor of snakes, nor the groundswell that heralds the mob.
The dark is a solace, and death is an overture.
I am only afraid
Of the cold dull lids of eyes,
And the cold dull grain of sand in the soul,
Indurate, insensate, not to be made incandescent
Even by God.
I am afraid of the stupid people.

(1920)

VENICE

The canals assimilate all life.
Time runs backward, sliding, mandragonal.
Six-tailed ripples like gonfalons float over underworlds.
Phosphorescence velvets the water like festival cloths dragged
    from gondolas;
Like churchyard mould, liquid with emerald rot.
All life is fluctuant in the canals, secret unseemly life.
Green plants, swarming on marble steps, grow animal,
    drowned fur, matted hair.

Venice at dawn, sly, macabre, eavesdropping out of the grave.
Venice under the stars, beauty of strong unholiness,
    manichaean, bowing before the powerful spirit of evil.
Venice at sunset (long red entrails dragged through the red
    canals),
Victim of dark archaic rituals with death as the climax—
What's the sense without death as the climax?
But an obstinate death of dreams.

This is the matrix, this is the secret workshop of life.
Lurching up to the surface, the undersoul rears itself
Out of the swift creative slime whence life,
Life and all beauty stems.

(c. 1934)

HOUSE

In the house that I shall make
Nothing must the wood forsake.
Cedars planing, laurels massing—
You will scarcely heed the passing
Of a threshold, for the posts
Lurk as reticent as ghosts,
And a skulking lintel sets
Fennel forth and violets,
And the hearth's contentment purrs
As its logs were in the firs.

When you go to take the air
Who will know and who will care
Outside comes and inside ends,
Interlocking, more than friends?
Chestnut-bark, uncoiled and sunk
In walls, so lately clasped a trunk,
And the smells of house and wood
Harbor such similitude.
As a heathen makes divine
His hall with one ancestral shrine,
In my midmost court shall be
An old benignant growing tree.

Death may come and doubtful stand,
Lift a latch and stay his hand.
Is this a lodge, is this a cave?
Why compose some other grave
When the mellowing place has grown
A reconcilement of its own,
And the tenant, moving slow
As dormant roots and seasons go
On to some more prosperous birth,
One already with the earth?

(1934)

TWO POEMS OF OLD AGE

EMBERS

Oh, the lean old woman, crouching in the fire,
　Fumbling in her bleared old heart to find the bitter truth:
All the fume of life is past, memories for a hearthstone last,
　Warming bones and marrow with the faggots of her
　youth.

"An' some was boys, an' some was dreams, an' some was
　devils from the Pit.
I loved 'em far as love could go—an' glad of it—an' glad of it!
A hundred—Lord, how long ago! I whisht' they'd been a
　hundred mo'!
　Love is all your hands kin hold."

Oh, the proud old woman, mumbling in the fire,
Like a king of Ninevah, of Lydia, or of Tyre,
　Flinging on her funeral pyre her purple and her gold.

THE OLD FISHERMAN

The old man troubled me, sitting so lax in the boat,
So fulfilled,
With that indrawn umbilicular look
Translating the centre of being
To terms of himself.
And his indolent line in the water,
A nerve outside of his body,
Keeping his touch on the pulse of the sea.

The old man sucked at his pipe,
Answered, "Uh-huh,"
Kindly, abstractedly, nothing to talk about—
He, an initiate.

(1926)

PART THREE

West Indian Poems
(*c.* 1940)

JEUNE FILLE OCTOROON

At the Sacré Coeur in Paris
They took me for white.
I sat with the daughters of ducs and maréchals.
One day Soeur Marie-Martre made us swear in the chapel
Never to work in a life class
Where the models went without robes.
We bathed in a chemise.

But the air of tonight
Is pressing against my body,
Insistent, harsh as a thorn-bush,
Saying, What can be this?
This is the enemy. This is between us.
And the Radi drums are abroad in this air,
Crying! Crying! Tearing the gauze of dusk
In the grove of the plunging shadows.

WARNING

Oh, do not be his sacrifice,
The lover who fondles you under the palms.
Tell him, You are my pleasure, I take you.
Do not say, I am yours.
All that you offer to gods or to lovers, as you offer to fire,
They take.
Do not burn yourself in his passion, insatiate, long-toothed.
When the gods love a worshipper too well
They devour him.

DUTY

Tread lightly.
Speak like the soft texture of magnolia
That bruises at one light graze to brown silence.
Be lovely, be invitation and calling to the touch,
Melt like the dance, swelling to graciousness.

Ti Phina is a good woman.
It squeezes her heart to be lavish but she doles to the church.
When her mouth-corner twists to abuse she forces kind words.
She wrings her kindness out of a sour heart-pulp
Like bitter cassava cakes.

But men do not love her.
The angels may love her
But surely they do not visit her.

LOVE SONG

Zozéphine!
Beat a woman all you want if you'll only love her.
Burn her caille over her head, swing her out of the door,
If you'll only pick her up and love her.
Zozéphine!
Come to the Danse Congo,
My blood is caught in my veins as the fish is caught in the net.
The seine of my veins all over my body is full of the struggle,
    the gasp and the anguish.
Don't be afraid.
    *Don' mind if I sharpen my claws on yo' hide, your smooth
        pulpy arms,*
    Same like a kitten on the banana trunk.
    Same like all married people.
Zozéphine, Zozéphine!
This man loves you plenty!

JUDGE ACHILLE FONTAINE

Folk-ways are final, supreme, holding the only authority;
Crystalized they are Law.
Our folk-ways now climb the peak
Like the peak of the *mornes*.
We wear long-tailed coats, we specialize forks,
We flatter Americans. Hé, we behave ourselves.
It is the law. It is right.

But one fine day, O Legba! O Dumballo!
The Radi drums shall shatter the Champ de Mars,
And the god who delights in death, in death with blood,
Whose name I dare not name—
(Or you or I should die in the year, but probably I)—
The only god of the blacks who has power over the whites,
That god would be sated!

He would pick his teeth,
He would droop his lids in the smug postprandial nap.
And the ancient ways, the ways of the ancient folk
They would be ours once more.
O Legba! O Dumballo! O Voodoo Pantheon!
Our folk-ways then would be Law.
They would be right.

THE SELFISH WOMAN

Love me or leave me alone.
You shall no longer cling about my lap,
Your love that will not love!
Your separateness that will not go away!
If you were gone
I could be all creation in myself.
But not with you to lead me and frustrate me—
Your hesitations, your half-tones, your cowardice.
I run the gauntlet like a savage captive,
Torn into ravellings
Not by the spears of men but by the gold pins of the women!

COMPENSATORY FIDELITY

The century-plant is noways swift to bloom
O Melinita!
Nor the love of a poor old man. . . .
But it will not blossom swiftly for another.

ADVICE FROM A MAMALOI

Too much virtue is unseemly
And unconducive to grace in the dance.
Throw a few crumbs to the devils,
Be a little to blame.
You sweet one! Lovely!
Would old Father God have been so anxious to save the world
If *it* had been soft and easy to tame?

ABORIGINAL

The queerest thing about Haiti—
(Said the American officer)
You'd think that a dark residium
Of primitive passion, nearer-to-nature impulse,
Lingered under the Frenchified eau-de-toilette
Of the inner circle?

Well, sir, I tell you, *c'est vé'itab.'*
Girls who were convent-bred, gentille, alluring,
Marry—yes, with a *dot.*

By Gad, sir. Maybe the primitive law of our nature—
Maybe the female apes
Came to the husband's tribe
Laden with calabash cups and coconuts,
Or else they died old maids.

ELEGY ON A LOVER

The night closed round him like a candle
But I was the flaming bud on the wick.
The waves of the air ebbed from him full of my pulses,
His thoughts swam in my blood,
Why should he know my secrets?
He turned my arteries inside out.
He rasped my heart with his nails
And my own eyes looked at me, under his wing-shaped
   eyebrows—
Woman-eyed! Horrible . . .
I am glad that he is dead.

SUCCESS

One man came to my caille,
Stood in the shade of the mango,
One night when I dance with my shadow.
His face was stupid and hard and distorted with love.
My breath died out in my throat
As though I were under the manchineel branches.
One night I told him, "You are my man.
You would not beat me."
I cooked him a pot of plantains,
With pepper, with fish and chicken.
Then memory woke in his eyes.
His dry ribs rattled like pods,
The smell of the earth came from him.
He ran—his fingers crooked to dig up the earth,
To hide in his grave.

               I thank, I thank old Legba!
I shall go dance in Port-au-Prince,
Make all the money!
Even the zombies, the zombies, the zombies
Come to stare at my dancing out of the grave.

PART FOUR

Three Early Poems

HALF-CONFESSIONS

Does the dusk bring you thoughts that are close yet remote,
With the startle and chill of a kiss in the throat?
Have you known the distemper of silence, disease
    Of solitude—devil that beats with its hands,
Sick to be drained of itself to the lees,
        Lost in the flux of the world that is rife
        Scarcely outside it; a need, not of life,
    Nay, but of death that itself understands.

Does your soul flush back other live souls as they pass,
    Hold perfect a moment their colour and form,
Yet feel them stopped short by—quicksilver and glass?
    Is your self like a hot-house, too troubled and warm,
Starred, half with exotics with agate-smooth claws,
    And sulphurous breathing, ophidian bark;
And half with the commonest daisies and haws,
    Whose petals and prickles are turned every one
        To yearn from this reeking, luxurious dark
    To the openings, covered with crystal and sun?

(1894?)

LIFE IN DEATH

A mouldered wall—worn stones against the sky
Unequal, gaping, like a toothless age;
Diseased with leprous scars of scaling white
And sucked with hungry parasites of moss
That dig the claws along the mortars' line;
Rank growth of grass, but choked with last year's dead,
Thick-sown with skeletons of poplar-leaves
Denuded, bared of green by gorging worms;
Keen spires struggling through the throttling vines
Or flattened close and sucking to the stones,
Untouched by light, in livid fleckiness;
A splendid, strangling shroud of threaded leaves,
Strong, savage tangles, succulent and wild,
Close vampire-vines, the scavengers of death,
That link in rank, deformed luxuriance
A blasted poplar, loathing, with the wall.—
The bridal of two corpses!
                                        Over all
Warm sunshine, welling from the mottled sky,
Flows fully, overwhelms, and fades again
In equal, rhythmic motion—like a pulse.

March 12th (1892?)

EGOTISM

I lie by your love embraced
  Like a slippery stone
In the flow of a runnel placed,
  Half-stolid, and senseless, and dreamily feeling alone
The lapping, lulling motion of your loving,
  So soft, so smooth, deliciously the same.—
  I cannot love, but constantly would claim
The folding flow, forever—ever—moving.

December 14th, 1890

CARL A. RUDISILL LIBRARY
LENOIR RHYNE COLLEGE

Text set in Baskerville linotype

*Composition, printing, and binding by
The Seeman Printery, Incorporated,
Durham, North Carolina*

*Sixty-pound Olde Style wove paper by S. D. Warren Company,
Boston, Massachusetts*

End paper drawing by George Kachergis

*Jacket and end paper printed by Meredith-Webb Printing
Company, Burlington, North Carolina, on eighty-pound, white
Strathmore Text*

*Designed and published by The University of North Carolina
Press, Chapel Hill, North Carolina*